RAILWAYS AROUND HEREFORD

Robert Lewis

AMBERLEY

Acknowledgements

I wish to thank Les Hyde and Phil Baldwin for letting me use their photographs, as well as Andy Baldwin, Norman Bishop and my railway enthusiast and non-railway enthusiast friends for the help and support they have given me while I wrote this book. I would also like to thank the staff at Amberley Publishing for their help and support. All photographs were taken by the author unless otherwise stated.

References

Smith, William H., *Herefordshire Railways* (1998).
Wood, Gordon, *Railways of Hereford* (2003).

First published 2018

Amberley Publishing
The Hill, Stroud
Gloucestershire, GL5 4EP

www.amberley-books.com

Copyright © Robert Lewis, 2018

The right of Robert Lewis to be identified as the Author of this work has been asserted in accordance with the Copyrights, Designs and Patents Act 1988.

ISBN 978 1 4456 8007 1 (print)
ISBN 978 1 4456 8008 8 (ebook)

British Library Cataloguing in Publication Data.
A catalogue record for this book is available from the British Library.

Origination by Amberley Publishing.
Printed in the UK.

Introduction

This book will cover railways around Hereford from the end of steam and the introduction of new traction in the mid-1960s right up to 2017, showing a big change in the railway scene not just around Hereford, but across the country. It has been hard to choose the photographs to put into the book as between myself, Les and Phil we have around 6,000 photographs taken around Hereford. I hope you will enjoy those included, which show the history, traction, locations and workings around Hereford from the mid-1960s to the present day, as of the time of writing.

Many of the locations where the historical photographs were taken are no longer available due to new buildings, fencing and the many trees that are now near the lineside. As a result, the book not only covers the traction and workings around Hereford, but also shows the changing landscape. I have not covered too much of the history of the railways around Hereford as there are many excellent books that have been published over the years which go into much more detail. Despite this, hopefully this book will provide a history of the railways around Hereford in photographs.

My interest in railways started in the mid-1970s, and as you can imagine other local railway enthusiasts and I have seen many changes in the railway scene in Hereford and the North and West Route, which is now known as the Marches Line, and the whole of the United Kingdom as a whole. As a boy of around eleven I moved to a house that backed onto the railway line just south of Hereford station, and I started to record the numbers of the trains and engines, and the workings and times of the trains that passed my home. Sadly, I no longer have these records to look back on.

Back then I think the highlight for me was on summer Saturdays, when the Marches Line used to have all the holiday specials from the South West to the North West and other locations with a mixed range of traction. The highlight for me was seeing the Newton Abbot to Stirling Motorail with all the cars and Mk 1 coaches. As I got a bit older, I started to go down to the station and meet other local railway enthusiasts, some of whom were of my age group, and we began to travel the railways. I am not sure if children of today's world would be allowed to travel to London on their own. Many of the friends I made back then are still friends today.

Hereford had a mix of passenger, parcel and freight workings back in the 1970s and 1980s. Bitumen tanks passed through Hereford and some of them would have been dropped off in the railyard for local use. Other freight workings, which would have also been dropped off, included Freightliners, cement, chemicals, clay slurry, motor vehicles from Speke (Liverpool), coal, fertilizer, steel, timber, SpeedLink services, British Oxygen Company tanks for South Wales and oil tanks for West Wales and for the small power station, which used oil for a while. The timber workings also passed through Hereford, with some going in to the railyard to be unloaded for lorries to take the timber to a local saw mill. Hereford also saw a good mix of railtours, both diesel, like the Merrymakers and railway enthusiasts' tours, and steam in the 1980s, with many of the steam engines being based at the Bulmer's Railway Centre or serviced there while the tour took a break. If a steam engine needs water today, it is provided in the station area.

On average there were around ten freight and parcels workings in the evening. One evening in particular stands out, however, when Hereford saw seventeen freight workings in one evening. Nowadays Hereford may not see seventeen freight workings in a week, but before my time and back in the heyday of the railways around 100 freight trains a day would pass through Hereford.

Apart from the variety of freight, passenger and parcel workings, Hereford had a variety of traction in the 1970s and 1980s, with Class 08s and 09s being based in Hereford for working around the station and railyard and for trips to Bulmer's. Additionally, Class 20s and 25s worked freight, parcels and passenger trains, while Class 31s, 37s and 45s worked just freight and passengers. Class 33s were mostly for passenger trains, while Class 40s were intended mainly for freight but also worked passenger workings and railtours few times. Class 47s were for mixed services and Class 50s worked the Paddington to Hereford services. Back then, if a passenger or freight train failed an engine was always close by. With so many varieties available to take over, diversity was always guaranteed.

The late 1980s and early 1990s to the mid-1990s saw the loco-hauled North and West Route services being replaced by DMU units and the loco-hauled services to and from Paddington being replaced by the high-speed train (HST). I did not take many photographs in the 1990s but I did start to record videos, and looking back at those videos there was a steady decline in the amount and type of traction working on the North and West Route. However, the Class 56s seem to have made more of an appearance on freight, running steel workings, and Class 37s and 47s were still common on parcels and some freight trains. It was an interesting time for photography due to all the new coloured liveries on the engine and units. The Hereford Rail Festival took place on 5 May 1991, with many railtours and the railyard being used for the public to view the visiting locomotives.

By the mid-1990s privatisation had started and in 1995 I left the railway scene for around ten years; as a result, I had no idea what was happening in the railways. I am glad to say, however, that Phil and Les still took some photographs in that time period to keep a record of the traction and workings until I took an interest in railways again.

When I returned to the scene the railway was a very different place, with private companies running both passenger and freight services, the railyard having closed and Network Rail planning to use the area to build a depot for staff and equipment. It took me a while to get used to all the new rolling stock and locomotives and the other changes that had taken place while I was away. Hereford still had a mix of freight with steel from Margam to Dee Marsh, a Freightliner from Crewe to Wentlooge, which has now stopped, stone from Moreton, coal trains from Portbury to Rugeley power station, which is now closed, and both engineer's and Network Rail test trains.

When I returned to the railways, traction mainly included Class 60s, 66s and 70s, but with Class 37s and 47s still making appearances, along with other types of engines that may be seen on railtours. Since I came back to the railways we have had new timber workings up to Chirk and a clay working from Exeter, which now sadly travels via Bromsgrove.

At the present time, the only regular daytime freight workings through Hereford are the steel trains from Margam to Dee Marsh, the tarmac workings from Moreton-on-Lugg, the timber and motor vehicle workings from Portbury to Mossend and the coal trains from Portbury to Fiddlers Ferry power station, but I am not sure how much longer that working will last. Timber still runs from Baglan Bay to Chirk, plus any other freight, and once in a while the Marches Line may get some diverted freight, such as the Tesco liner.

Night-time freight workings booked to run are from Carlisle to Margam, Mossend to Cardiff Tidal, Onllwyn Washery to Scunthorpe, Cwmbargoed to Hope, and stone from Moreton.

The Marches Line also sees short-term and as-required freight workings with a mix of both steam and diesel railtours tours plus Network Rail test trains and engineer's trains. If you use the internet, more up-to-date information about freight and passenger railtours can be found by using websites like Realtime Trains.

With new franchises being awarded for services through Hereford and the promise of new trains and new train operating companies, I am looking forward to adding more types of traction to my collection of photographs. If you would like to view the many other photographs taken around Hereford, and to keep updated on the railways, then please have a look at the following Flickr pages: railhereford, Redhill Bull and hydey44.

No. 6847 is seen passing Holmer on 11 May 1965 with what appears to be an empty steel working heading north. The Henry Wiggins steel mill is on the right-hand side, and right up to the early 1980s a freight working of tanks used to go into the mill. Sadly this view is no longer available, like many other views of the lineside, due to trees and buildings. (Les Hyde)

D1661 *North Star* and D1726 leave the station on 4 June 1965 with a passenger working. D1661 is now preserved on the West Somerset Railway while D1726 is now with Direct Rail Services, running under the number 47841. (Les Hyde)

A busy scene with two mixed van freights in the station. The driver of D7070 is waving to the signalman as he is about to pass the signal box at the north end of Platform 2 with a mixed freight on 10 May 1967. Apart from freight workings, Hymeks also worked the Paddington to Hereford services after steam left the route. After the Hymeks, doubled-headed Class 31s worked the services from London until the Class 47s and Class 50s took over. (Les Hyde)

D6976 is seen at Redhill Junction after travelling on the line from Barton with a mixed freight heading for South Wales on 31 May 1964. (Les Hyde)

A DMU is seen passing the then closed Redhill Junction signal box. (Les Hyde)

D7024 receives the fitters' attention at Barton shed in 1964. (Les Hyde)

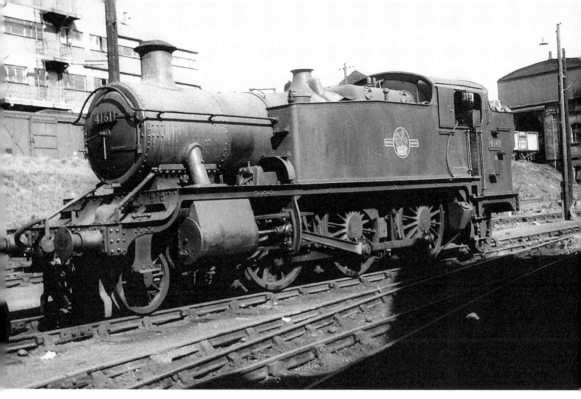

No. 4161, a Class 2-6-2T Prairie, is seen in Barton Yard in 1964. One of its duties was to work the Hereford to Gloucester via Ross-on-Wye services just before the line closed in November 1964. Another local line that closed in 1964 was the Hereford to Brecon line; it had closed to passenger services in 1962, but closed completely in 1964. At one time Barton Yard had around 400 staff working there. (Les Hyde)

No. 6876 *Kingsland Grange* is seen passing Grafton, south of Hereford, in April 1964 with a mixed freight working heading for Redhill Junction, where it could have taken the freight-only line to Barton or the line to Hereford station. I am pleased to say that you can still take photographs from this location today. (Les Hyde)

Class 04 0-6-0 shunter D2219, built by Drewry Car Co. Ltd in about 1954, is seen in Barton Yard in 1964. D2219 was a Hereford-based shunter for a short while from 28 August to 29 November 1964; it was then transferred to Worcester. The houses in the background are still standing, but where D2219 is seen stabled there is now a supermarket car park. (Les Hyde)

A three-car Swindon DMU passing Holmer, Hereford, on 11 May 1965 with a Hereford to Birmingham working. (Les Hyde)

D1586 waiting to leave Barton Yard with a freight working of vans in 1964. (Les Hyde)

A view of the station on 15 June 1967 with D1741 waiting to leave with a passenger working. The Down freight line, which can be seen in this photograph, was lifted in the summer of 1969, but was then replaced in 1973.

Nos 73019 and 70026 *Polar Star* and D1698 are seen passing through the station on 14 April 1967. Both No. 73019 and No. 70026 were heading for scrapyards in South Wales. (Les Hyde)

A rare photograph of a train working the freight-only Barton Yard to Redhill Junction line passing through Newton Farm. D1641, which was a Landore-based engine at the time, is seen on a mixed freight heading for Redhill Junction on 2 June 1966. The line from Barton to Redhill Junction is now a foot and cycle path and the flats in the background have been knocked down. (Les Hyde)

Barrs Court Junction signal box in the early 1950s. The local railway enthusiasts called this spot the Perch; another name was the Kop. (Les Hyde)

D856 *Trojan* passing Redhill with a North West to Plymouth passenger working in 1964. Around 1970 the North West to South West workings were rerouted via Birmingham New Street and a new Crewe to Cardiff working started, which was worked by DMUs and then later on by Class 25s. (Les Hyde)

D1587 waits for a crew change at the station on 2 June 1967 while working down to South Wales. (Les Hyde)

Crew change time for D1551, which, based at Tinsley, was working a northbound parcels working on 29 May 1965. The photograph was taken from the signal box at the end of the platform. (Les Hyde)

D856 *Vigilant* and D1654 are seen stabled on 10 April 1968. (Les Hyde)

D1650, an Old Oak Common-based engine, is seen passing the then closed Redhill Junction signal box on 8 February 1967 with a northbound passenger working from Barrs Court station. The line heading off to the right ran down the freight-only line through Newton Farm and Hunterdon to Barton Yard and re-joined the main line at Barrs Court Junction. (Les Hyde)

D6990, seen stabled at the Aylestone Hill bridge end of the station on 20 August 1966. (Les Hyde)

D1918 runs through Barrs Court station with a freight working on 2 June 1967. (Les Hyde)

D1604, having just come from the station, is seen at Redhill Junction with a southbound passenger working in the mid-1960s. The line to the left would have taken you down to Barton Yard, and re-joined the main line again at Barrs Court Junction. (Les Hyde)

D1652 waiting to leave the station on 17 September 1966 with a mixed freight. (Les Hyde)

D1681 arriving in Barrs Court station on 10 May 1967 with a passenger working. (Les Hyde)

No. 25221 is seen leaving Hereford with the 10.00 Crewe to Cardiff Central on 15 November 1977. Class 25s worked the North and West Route from about 1975 until around 1981, when the Class 33s started to take over. (Les Hyde)

No. 46030 leaving Hereford with a mixed van working heading for South Wales on 4 November 1977. Class 46s on the North and West Route were not uncommon around this time, working both freight and passengers. (Les Hyde)

No. 24087 is seen waiting to leave Hereford station with the 06.15 Crewe to Cardiff Central on 3 November 1977. No. 24087 replaced a failed engine north of Hereford. (Les Hyde)

No. 50009 *Conqueror* is seen reversing an ECS from Platform 2 over to Platform 3 to then work the 16.30 Hereford to London Paddington on 4 May 1981. This photograph takes me back to when I was a teenager, when the evening trains would arrive in Hereford from Paddington to be stabled overnight. My friends and I would wait to see if we could have a cab ride down to the diesel sidings, and on occasion we would drive the trains down to the sidings and walk back up to the station, and on the way have a visit to the signal box – all under supervision of the driver. I am not sure what health and safety would make of it in today's world. (Les Hyde)

No. 25231 is seen passing Grafton, south of Hereford, on 3 June 1983 with the 3V20 Manchester to Bristol parcels. (Les Hyde)

No. 40143 is seen waiting to leave Hereford station on 22 April 1983 with an oil tank working. (Les Hyde)

A busy Hereford station on 29 April 1981 sees No. 25245 waiting to leave with the 17.10 Cardiff Central to Crewe and No. 50021 waiting to cross over from Platform 2 to Platform 3 to work the 18.45 Hereford to London Paddington. (Les Hyde)

No. 25224 arrives at Hereford with the 17.10 Cardiff Central to Crewe on 4 June 1981. The timetable around this time was for six Crewe to Cardiff passenger services each way per day. In the timetable for 2017, there are around thirty-two passenger services each way from West Wales to Manchester and from Cardiff to Holyhead and North Wales. (Les Hyde)

No. 33110 passes Redhill and is about to pass under the A49 road bridge with the 13.07 Cardiff Central to Crewe on 23 March 1982. As far as I know only a handful of Class 331s worked passenger workings on the North and West Route, and once in a while the Marches Line used to see Class 332s working services. (Les Hyde)

In the 1970s and the 1980s the North and West Route used to have summer Saturday workings from the South West, and on 15 August 1981 No. 47324 is seen passing Grafton with the 09.48 Paignton to Liverpool Lime Street. One of the services that worked from South Wales was a Motorail with Mark 1 coaches, which I can remember passing the bottom of my garden. In the summer of 1997 there was a short-lived summer Saturday working via the Marches from Penzance to Manchester. (Les Hyde)

No. 47585 *County of Cambridgeshire*, as well as Nos C394, T042 and T039, are stabled on the refuelling point on 3 June 1990. (Les Hyde)

Nos 37084, 37906, 37411, 47476 and 37428 are stabled under the wall on 20 August 1988. I am not sure if Cardiff Canton would have as many engines stabled there today as there are in this photograph. (Les Hyde)

Nos 31411 and 31437 passing Grafton on 19 June 1992 with the Fridays-only 16.40 Cardiff Central to Manchester. (Les Hyde)

Nos 20081 and 20016 are seen leaving Hereford on 27 April 1990 with the 1Z40 Sheffield to Bristol Temple Meads railtour. (Les Hyde)

No. 47403 stands in Hereford railyard on 30 December 1992. No. 47403 was withdrawn in 1986 and was then on loan to the Ministry of Defence at the RAOC camp at Moreton-on-Lugg as a training aid for the SAS. No. 47403 was moved from Hereford to Toton in February 1993. (Les Hyde)

No. 37702 is seen arriving in Hereford on 8 January 1987 with a mixed freight. Nos 20155 and 20158 had worked a freight as far as Hereford a few days before and were waiting to work back up north. (Les Hyde)

No. 150242 under the wall with a crew training working on 16 April 1987. (Les Hyde)

English, Welsh & Scottish (EWS) No. 60042 *Hundred of Hoo* is seen waiting to leave with an MGR to South Wales on 8 August 2003. EWS became DB in 2009. (Les Hyde)

E3003 and No. 50027 *Lion* are stabled in the bay on 18 June 1994. E3003 was on display at Worcester open day and was waiting to be moved back north. (Les Hyde)

No. 40028 is photographed leaving Hereford with the 1Z36 Leeds to Cardiff Central 'Christmas Cracker' railtour on 17 December 1983. (Phil Baldwin)

No. 33027 *Earl Mountbatten of Burma* passes Wellington crossing with the 1V07 Crewe to Cardiff Central on 7 July 1986. (Phil Baldwin)

No. 50022 *Anson* passing Stoke Edith with the 1B40 London Paddington to Hereford on 2 August 1987. (Phil Baldwin)

No. 25034 arrives in Hereford with a mineral wagon working on 18 September 1986. (Phil Baldwin)

No. 47449 with a northbound ICI chemical tank working on 14 August 1988. (Phil Baldwin)

Nos 20131 and 20124 make a very rare sight on the 3V20 Manchester to Bristol Temple Meads parcels, leaving Hereford on 18 June 1988. This is another view that is no longer available due to overgrown trees. (Phil Baldwin)

No. 47291 *The Port of Felixstowe* is captured waiting to leave Hereford on 17 May 1988 with the 6V65 Ravenhead Junction to West Wales oil tanks. (Phil Baldwin)

No. 33006 passes Redhill on 12 June 1986 with the 1V09 Crewe to Cardiff Central. (Phil Baldwin)

Nos 37037 and 37099 are seen passing Holmer with the 6S50 Llanwern to Mossend steel coil on 25 May 1992. (Phil Baldwin)

No. 50037 is seen passing Holmer on 10 April 1988 with the 1B33 London Paddington to Hereford. (Phil Baldwin)

Nos 31461 and 31174 are seen passing Brecon curve with the Fridays-only 1M89 Cardiff Central to Manchester on 24 July 1992. (Phil Baldwin)

No. 25300 is captured leaving Hereford with the Moreton-on-Lugg to Severn Tunnel Junction on 20 March 1985. Apart from looking back at old photographs of railway workings, I think it's also nice to look back at the cars that were on the roads at that time, as in the background.

No. 25059 eases its train of southbound ICI tanks out of Brecon Curve loop on a foggy day on 30 November 1985. (Phil Baldwin)

On a lovely summer's evening, No. 31410 is seen passing over the River Wye with a short 3V20 Manchester to Bristol Temple Meads working on 23 July 1989. Local fishermen used the bridge as a shortcut to cross over to the other side of the river; nowadays there is now a foot and bike bridge for people to use.

No. 6000 *King George V* is seen at the Bulmer's Railway Centre on 12 July 1987. *King George V* was based at the Bulmer's Railway Centre for many years and on Sunday mornings I enjoyed having rides behind the *King* at the Centre. The bell on the front of the engine was presented by the Baltimore Ohio Railroad Company when the loco went over to the USA in 1927. In 1971, *King George V* became the first steam locomotive to travel on BR rails since the ban in 1969. The loco worked many railtours from Hereford and the rest of the UK and is now on display at the museum of the Great Western Railway in Swindon.

After No. 31252 failed at Hereford station, and with No. 50040 the only engine stabled in Hereford at that time, it was put on to work down to South Wales with a long welded rail working on 19 May 1989.

No. 31117 is seen waiting to leave Hereford with a short working from the Royal Army Ordnance Corps depot in Moreton-on-Lugg to Severn Tunnel Junction on 18 June 1985. There was a working from the RAOC most days of the week, with a variety of locomotives over the years. The RAOC closed in the early 2000s and is now a business park.

Nos 25269 and 25262 make a rare sight of Class 25s working steel coils for South Wales on a cold and wet night on 6 December 1985.

Ex-works No. 47533 passes Holmer with a southbound passenger on 8 July 1987.

No. 08932 leaves Bulmer's and heads for the railyard on 4 March 1988. The vans would have been picked up later that day by the 6S74 SpeedLink from Cardiff Tidal to Mossend. It is hard to believe, looking at this photograph, but there was a double track at this location. Trains to and from Brecon would bear off at this point and the line to Barton and Redhill Junction would carry straight on.

A photograph taken from the old footbridge that crossed over the line of No. 08932 heading for the railyard from Bulmer's on 4 March 1988. The bridge that can be seen in the background is carrying the A49 to Leominster. The track is still in place but the line is now very overgrown with trees and is no longer linked to the main line. The Class 08 would bear to the right and cross over Burcott Road level crossing to gain access to the railyard for the oil tanks to be picked up by a main line diesel; the track which you can see going straight on in the background on would have carried on to join the main line at Barrs Court signal box and junction, but by the time this photograph was taken this part of the line was disused.

Cider Queen is seen giving brake van rides around Bulmer's Railway Centre on 12 July 1987. *Cider Queen* is now running as D2578 and is preserved by the D2578 Locomotive Group at Morton Park, where it moved from Bulmer's in August 2001. D2578 became the first privately owned diesel to run on the main line when it worked a brake van special from Hereford to the RAOC at Moreton-on-Lugg in July 1971.

Nos 40057 and 40135 are captured leaving Hereford on 28 May 1984 with the 1Z36 'Devonia' railtour from Preston to Paignton.

Nos 51512, 59093 and 51500 are seen waiting in Hereford for their next working on 16 August 1984.

Heading for South Wales on 14 April 1989, No. 37133 is about to pass under the college bridge with a long welded rail working. Much would have changed in the background if you were to compare this image to a photograph taken at the same spot today.

No. 50019 *Ramillies* is photographed heading for Shelwick Junction on 26 June 1988 with a Hereford to London Paddington. It's hard to place this photograph nowadays as it was taken from the Roman road bridge and all the buildings to the left have been demolished and to the right of No. 50019 there are now car showrooms.

No. 47111 was hit while stationary at Preston station by a two-car DMU. The photograph shows No. 47111 in Hereford on 22 March 1986 prior to being moved to Canton, where it was cut up in 1987.

No. 33001 waits to leave the station on 4 October 1985 with a PW working. I am not sure why No. 33001 was on this working but as far as I know it was the only time a Class 33 worked a PW in the Hereford area.

Time for a new driver for No. 47309 on 16 May 1989, which was working a mixed freight – possibly the 6S74 Cardiff Tidal to Mossend. Meanwhile, two local railway enthusiasts, whom I have known for many years, are in deep conversation.

No. 33056 *The Burma Star* makes a rare sight on a steel coil train waiting to leave on 9 April 1985 with a Dee Marsh to South Wales working. No. 33056 was withdrawn in 1991 and was sent to the Ludgershall & Churnet Valley Railway for preservation but was cut up in 2006.

No. 33113 with 4TCs Nos 404 and 420 passing the former station at St Devereux on 26 April 1986 with the 1Z30 London Waterloo to Hereford charter.

Nos 25249 and 25296 leave Hereford on 23 May 1984 with the 6V32 Ellesmere Port to Severn Tunnel Junction bitumen tanks.

D9000 *The Royal Scots Grey* is seen in Hereford station on 17 October 1987. I have no records or any other information to say why D9000 was in Hereford.

Nos 47575 and 33001 arriving in Hereford on 26 June 1985 with the 1M70 Swansea to Manchester; No. 47575 was removed at Hereford and named *City of Hereford*.

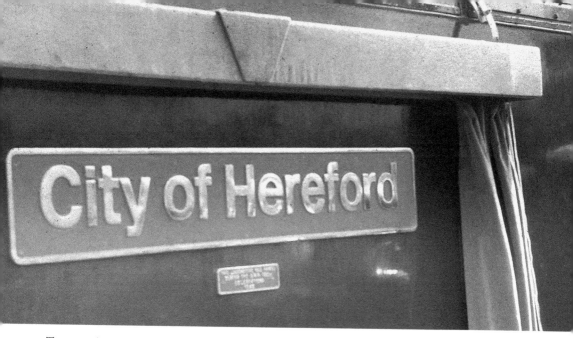

The nameplate of No. 47575 *City of Hereford*, which was, rather aptly, named at Hereford station on 26 June 1985. Apart from No. 47575, other locomotives that have a link to Hereford are LMS Coronation Class No. 46225, GWR County Class 4-6-0 steam locomotive No. 1017 *County of Hereford*, GWR Castle Class steam locomotive No. 7022 *Hereford Castle*, No. 47207 *Bulmers of Hereford*, which was named at Hereford station on 1 December 1987, and No. 31405, which was named *Mappa Mundi* at Hereford Rail Festival in May 1991 after the thirteenth-century map of the world which is on display in Hereford Cathedral. The nameplate from No. 31405 was later transferred to No. 47767 for a short while and is now on display in Hereford Cathedral.

No. 47628 is seen leaving Hereford with a Hereford to London Paddington working on 20 April 1985.

No. 31434 is seen leaving Hereford with a Hereford to Birmingham New Street working on 19 April 1989.

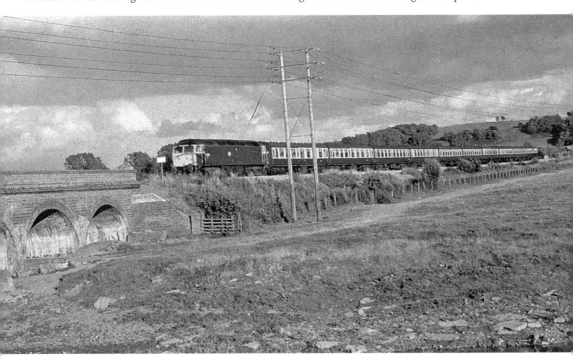

No. 47535 is about to cross over the River Wye to the south of Hereford station with a South Wales to North West working on 20 June 1985. Just to the south was the Rotherwas signal box, which served Rotherwas Junction, where trains to Ross-on-Wye would have left the main line. Rotherwas was also the site of the Royal Ordnance Filling Factory, where around 6,000 workers in both world wars filled bombs, with a layout of around 27 miles of railway inside of the factory, trains and its own small station. Trains brought workers in from the local area and took bombs back out by rail. There is now a footbridge crossing over the river at this point. It is a shame that you can no longer take a photograph from this spot due to all the trees that have grown in the area.

Nos 51369, 59521 and 51411 are photographed passing the signal box on 22 September 1985.

No. 47322 is about to cross over the River Wye with a working of wagons on 8 February 1988.

Nos 33053 and 33047 *Spitfire* are seen passing Redhill, about 2 miles south of Hereford, on 5 May 1991. Nos 33053 and 33047 worked the 1Z40 'The Border Flyer' railtour from Basingstoke to Hereford for the Hereford Rail Festival, so I would think this would be the return journey from Hereford to Basingstoke.

On a lovely summer's evening, Nos 37238 and 37271 are seen passing Brecon Curve on 24 July 1992 with the 4S81 Pengam to Coatbridge Freightliner. It was nice to see Class 37s on back on this working again as Class 56s were normally on the 4S81. (Phil Baldwin)

A busy Hereford station on 18 September 1991 with Nos 37412 and 37411 leaving with the 6S55 Burngullow to Irvine clay slurry, while Nos 37099 and 37520 wait to leave with a Llanwern to Dee Marsh steel coil. In the background a Class 47 waits to move on an ECS to the diesel sidings. (Phil Baldwin)

No. 56033, working the 4S81 Pengram to Coatbridge Freightliner, is seen waiting to leave on 23 September 1988.

Above: Nos 37675 and 37670 are passing the Folly trading estate to the south of the station on 12 April 1989 with the 6S55 Burngullow to Irvine clay tanks.

Opposite above: No. 45001 arrives in to Hereford station on 12 April 1985 with a ballast working.

Opposite below: No. 33052 *Ashford* arriving in Hereford with a Crewe to Cardiff Central working on 25 November 1984. In the background the Painter Brothers testing towers and the gasometer tower can be seen.

No. 37430 *Cwmbran* is seen just south of the station with a North West to Cardiff passenger working on 28 December 1988. This photograph was taken from the bottom of the garden of the house in which I lived at the time.

Nos 55930, 54400 and 55995 are seen leaving Hereford on 11 July 1990 with a parcels working. A year later the background would start to change, with new houses being built.

No. 150106 is captured leaving on what I would think would be a training special on 8 June 1986.

No. 156402 leaves Hereford on 5 April 1987. The trees in the foreground have now grown to block this view of the station. Rockfield DIY and the Post Office sorting office are no longer standing.

Above: No. 26038 is seen stabled on 4 May 1991. The next day, No. 26038 took part in the Hereford Rail Festival.

Opposite above: No. 153327 is seen leaving Hereford on 16 May 1988 with a Cardiff Central to Holyhead service. The Class 153s took over the loco-hauled services on the North and West Route, and I think the 153 also worked some services from Hereford to Oxford for a while.

Opposite below: No. 55033 is seen heading out from Bulmer's on 5 May 1991. This loco travelled from Hereford railyard to Bulmer's with shuttles for most of the day in connection with the Hereford Rail Festival. This photograph was taken from the A49 road bridge, so much has changed today, with buildings gone and, while the track is still on the ground, it is now very overgrown, so I cannot see any rail services ever working on this line again. The track was part of the route to the old Moorfields and Barton stations.

A very busy scene on 17 July 1990 with Nos 37694 and 37693 working a lime working from Margam to Tunstead, a Class 37 passing by with a scrap working for Cardiff Tidal and another Class 37 waiting to leave the station with a Dee Marsh to Llanwern steel working – a scene that I think will never happen again. The Mark 1 coaches were waiting to be removed from the railyard after being used as a training aid by the SAS at the Moreton-on-Lugg MOD camp.

No. 56032 *Sir De Morgannwg/County of South Glamorgan* is captured in Hereford railyard on 6 May 1991 with a working of mixed wagons. I have no information to say what the working was or why it was stabled in that part of the railyard. Not in view but still standing is the old goods shed, which is now being used as a bowling alley, and the buildings to the left have now been demolished to make way for a link road from the A49 to the A465, which comes out near the station. The railyard is now being used as a Network Rail depot for staff and equipment.

Nos 37294 and 37220 are seen passing the signal box, heading for West Wales on 8 August 1990 with the regular working of empty oil tanks.

No. 37049 passes Stoke Edith, heading for Ledbury on 19 May 1990 with a Hereford to London Paddington working. No. 37049 was put on at Hereford after the booked Class 47 or 50 failed before the start of the service, and I think the loco worked as far as Worcester or Oxford. Class 37s often worked the Hereford to Paddington service when the booked Class 47 or 50 failed on a Sunday afternoon.

D7523, D1842, D120 and No. 37414 stand in the station on 4 May 1991. The engines all came to Hereford to take part in the Hereford Rail Festival, which was on 5 May 1991.

No. 50015 *Valiant* is seen leaving Hereford on 5 May 1991 with a railtour from Hereford to Worcester Shrub Hill for the Hereford Rail Festival.

A smart-looking No. 37899 and No. 37698 are seen leaving Hereford on 6 May 1991. The parcel vans and the Travelling Post Office vans had been on show at the Hereford Rail Festival.

Two Rail Express Systems Class 47s make a colourful sight leaving Hereford in the early 1990s with a mixed rake of southbound parcels vans. Over the years Hereford has seen a range of traction on parcel workings.

Nos 31530 and 31270 are photographed arriving in the station on 17 July 1992 with the 5V89 Liverpool Edge Hill to Cardiff ECS, which worked back up from Cardiff to Manchester Oxford Road as the 1V89.

With another Class 37 arriving in the station, No. 37258 is seen in the early 1990s with an engineering train.

No. 37261 and another Class 37 are seen leaving Hereford in the late 1980s/early 1990s with the 4S81 Pengram to Coatbridge Freightliner.

No. 25309 is captured leaving Hereford on 17 September 1985 with an empty coal working heading for the North. (Phil Baldwin)

Nos 25059 and 25089 pass Burcott, north of Hereford station, on 6 September 1985 with the 6S74 Severn Tunnel Junction to Mossend working. (Phil Baldwin)

No. 45040 is seen in Hereford railyard with a ballast working on 18 April 1986. (Phil Baldwin)

No. 47286 stands in Hereford railyard on 11 April 1988 with the 6S74 Cardiff Tidal to Mossend. (Phil Baldwin)

No. 20904, with No. 20901 at the rear, passes Stoke Edith while heading to Ledbury on 10 October 1989 with a weed killer train. (Phil Baldwin)

No. 37701 is seen leaving Hereford on 21 March 1987 with the 6V07 Ellesmere Port to Pantyffynnon empty Cawoods coal. The Cawoods containers would carry coal from South Wales for shipment to Ireland. (Phil Baldwin)

No. 33049 makes a rare appearance on a steel coil working from Dee Marsh to South Wales in 1985. (Phil Baldwin)

In one of the photographs Phil and I had taken of Class 37s on passenger services on the Marches Line, No. 37422 makes a fine sight, complete with the Highland Terrier on its bodyside, as it coasts under the bridge heading for the station on 13 May 1989 with the 1V11 Manchester to Cardiff. Class 374s took over from the Class 33s and Mark 2 coaches began to be used on the services on the North and West Route. The regular Class 374s that worked passenger services were Nos 37426 to 37431, but others worked services as well, and freight Class 37s were not uncommon. Much has changed in the background, with new housing and the addition of a gas tower, and the towers of Printer Brothers have been removed. (Phil Baldwin)

Class 117 DMU T305 Nos 51410, 59520 and 51368 are seen passing the Bridge Inn, Holmer, with a Hereford to Birmingham New Street working in the 1990s. (Phil Baldwin)

A smart ex-works No. 56052 is seen arriving in Hereford station on 16 May 1989 with the 4S81 Pengam to Coatbridge Freightliner. (Phil Baldwin)

A busy railyard on 7 September 1988 with No. 37015 waiting to leave with the 6S74 Cardiff Tidal to Mossend. The timber was waiting to be collected by lorry to be taken down to Pontrilas Timber and the vans would have come from Bulmer's. (Phil Baldwin)

Nos 33010 and 33204 arrive from Cheltenham Spa on 19 March 1987 with the VOSO ECS, which would have worked from London with passengers to attend Cheltenham Races. After being cleaned, the train would have worked back to Cheltenham Spa to take the passengers back to London. (Phil Baldwin)

No. 47207 *Bulmers of Hereford* is seen in Hereford on 1 August 1988 with the 6S74 Cardiff Tidal to Mossend train. No. 47207 was named in Hereford station on 1 December 1987 and the nameplate was removed in March 1994. (Phil Baldwin)

No. 50017 *Royal Oak* is seen near Withington, heading for Ledbury with the 1A41 Hereford to London Paddington on 5 October 1986. (Phil Baldwin)

No. 31419 makes a rare sight at Redhill Curve on 10 October 1989 with the 1V08 Manchester Piccadilly to Cardiff Central working. (Phil Baldwin)

No. 37887 is about to pass under the College Road bridge on 3 October 1988 with the 6V07 Ellesmere Port to Pantyffynnon Cawoods empty coal. This was just one of the many photographs that Phil and I have taken of this working. (Phil Baldwin)

Nos 37674 and 37412 are seen passing Moreton-on-Lugg with the 6S55 Burngullow to Irvine china clay on 15 April 1992. (Phil Baldwin)

No. 40135 makes a rare sight on 15 June 1984 with the 6V64 Alban to Waterston oil tanks. (Phil Baldwin)

No. 45034 makes an unusual sight waiting to leave the station on 4 July 1985 with the 6V82 oil tanks to Robeston. (Phil Baldwin)

No. 45060 *Sherwood Forester* is captured leaving the station on 7 June 1985 with the 1V03 Crewe to Cardiff Central. Peaks were not a common sight on passenger workings on the North and West Route, so I am not sure how No. 45060 found its way on to this working. (Phil Baldwin)

A Class 08 heading into Bulmer's with an oil tank working in the late 1980s or early 1990s for the small power station that served the Bulmer's and Sun Valley factories before the power station stopped using oil and moved over to gas. (Phil Baldwin)

No. 47575 *City of Hereford* in Rail Express Systems livery with two Travelling Post Office coaches arrives in Hereford with an unidentified northbound parcels in 1991. Seeing the TPO coaches takes me back to when the Cardiff Central to Crewe TPO called at Hereford. It arrived in Hereford around 21.20 and it was always a busy scene at the station, with Royal Mail staff coming from the sorting office across the road and loading the bags of mail onto the TPO ready for the onboard staff to sort on its journey north. There was a Mark 1 corridor brake passenger coach in the formation so friends and I used to travel to Crewe and do an overnighter, watching the sleepers and all of the Royal Mail trains. When we used to go to London we would get up very early and travel on the southbound TPO, which left Hereford for Newport at about 03.45 a.m., for an early HST to Paddington. From May 1988 the Cardiff to Crewe became the Cardiff to York TPO, and over the years I have seen Class 37s, 45s, 47s and 50s work the service. I am not sure when the TPO service ended on the Marches Line, but all TPOs stopped in early January 2004.

No. 47407 passes Redhill Curve with the 1V18 Manchester Piccadilly to Cardiff Central on 7 July 1988. (Phil Baldwin)

No. 31448 passes Whitestone, heading for Hereford with a Birmingham to Hereford working on 29 September 1989. Class 31s replaced DMUs for about six months in 1989 due to a lack of DMUs. (Phil Baldwin)

With bashers in the front coach, No. 47716 *The Duke of Edinburgh's Award* is seen passing Stoke Edith while heading for Hereford with the 1B48 London Paddington to Hereford on 8 July 1990. (Phil Baldwin)

No. 60009 *Carnedd Dafydd* is seen leaving the station, heading for South Wales with a steel working on 14 May 1992. This view is now blocked by trees and the background has also changed, with the Royal Mail sorting office no longer there. (Phil Baldwin)

No. 60005 *Skiddaw* arrives in the station with a railtour from Shrewsbury rail open day on 30 May 1993. (Phil Baldwin)

In a fairly typical scene in Hereford on a Sunday in the 1980s we see No. 37177 on a southbound engineer's, No. 47509 stabled on a Hereford to London Paddington, No. 47533 waiting to leave with the 1M84 Cardiff Central to Crewe and Nos 47317 and 47241 stabled in the bay. This photograph was taken on 12 August 1984. (Phil Baldwin)

No. 47500 *Great Western* is seen arriving in Hereford with the 5A80 Old Oak to Hereford ECS on 5 July 1987. (Phil Baldwin)

Nos 37517 and 37518 pass Redhill Curve with a southbound cement working on 14 July 1997. (Phil Baldwin)

Passing Moreton-on-Lugg, Loadhaul No. 56034 *Ogmore Castle* and No. 56090 make light work of the 6M58 Carmarthen to Dee Marsh Junction empty timber working in the summer of 1997. (Phil Baldwin)

With the local horse looking on, No. 4936 *Kinlet Hall* makes a fine sight in the winter landscape near Tram Inn as it heads to South Wales with the 1Z40 Stratford-upon-Avon to Newport on 30 December 2000. (Phil Baldwin)

Sadly, the only photograph I can put into the book of a Western around Hereford is of D1015 passing Holmer on 5 May 2003 with the 1Z31 Castle Cary to Llandudno Junction Mendip Rail-Foster Hanson rail charter. Westerns also worked the Paddington to Hereford services for a while. (Phil Baldwin)

DB Schenker No. 60074 *Teenage Spirit* passes Coedmor, just north of Tram Inn, with the 6V75 Dee Marsh to Margam empty steel wagons on 1 June 2012. I am glad to say that you can still get photographs looking both ways from this location without it being affected by too many trees close to the lineside.

No. 175112 is seen passing Shelwick Junction on 1 September 2012 with a service from South Wales to North Wales or Manchester. The former Shelwick Junction signal box would have been on the right-hand side and the line to the left is to Ledbury and Worcester. Arriva Trains Wales, which is part of the DB Group, has had the franchises for Wales and the Marches Line since December 2003. In October 2017 Arriva withdrew from the tendering process, leaving three companies in the bidding for the new franchise, which is due to start in October 2018. Over the past fifteen years in which Arriva has held the franchise, the Marches Line has seen Class 142/143s (a few times on the Sunday morning working from Hereford), 150/2s, 158s, 175s and 57s with Mark 2 coaches and Class 67s with Mark 3 coaches working the Holyhead to Cardiff premier services, known as the WAG.

Nos 153365 and 170510 are seen leaving Hereford with the 18.48 Hereford to Birmingham New Street service on 31 August 2010. London Midland has held the franchise for the West Midlands, which covers Birmingham New Street to Hereford, and services to London Euston and Liverpool since November 2007, but in October 2017 it lost the franchise to West Midlands Trains, which is owned by Abellio, and which started to work the franchise in December 2017. Since London Midland has been running services between Birmingham New Street and Hereford the route has seen Class 150s, 153s, 170s and 172s, but in the main it has been the Class 170s that have been working the route.

No. 6201 *Princess Elizabeth* is seen passing Haywood, south of Hereford station, on the Royal Train with Her Majesty the Queen and the Duke of Edinburgh on board for a visit to Hereford on 11 July 2012. No. 6201 was based at the Bulmer's Railway Centre from 1976 to 1993.

No. 60163 *Tornado* is in blue when seen passing Grafton on a very wet and dull day on 24 November 2012 with the 1Z33 London Paddington to Shrewsbury. I don't think the dog was too happy to be out walking in the rain and was looking to get back home in the warm and dry. This was one of the first photographs to be taken from the then new bike/footpath.

Nos 66139, 66113, 66130 and 66059 pass Grafton on a very cold winter's day on 19 January 2013 with the 6M60 Exeter Riverside to Bescot clay tanks. This working was a way of getting engines back up to Bescot so to see two to four engines was not uncommon.

No. 66509 passes the College Road bridge with the Westbury to Tunstead cement tanks on 27 August 2010. This working has only ran a few times.

No. 70004 passes Redhill Curve on 12 July 2011 with the 6M55 Portbury to Rugeley power station coal train. Rugeley power station is now closed.

Nos 20312 and 20308 are seen passing Coedmor, just north of Tram Inn, with the 1Z29 Huddersfield to Swansea railtour on 27 April 2013.

No. 56133 passes Haywood with the 6Z66 Llanwern to Crewe CS on 19 June 2014

No. 66570 passes Moreton-on-Lugg on 3 March 2012 with the 4V64 Crewe Basford Hall to Wentlooge Freightliner. Just north of the signal box are the sidings into Moreton Park, where the stone empties are filled for the tarmac workings. The former station at Moreton was famous for its booking office, which was situated in a hollow oak tree. Moreton is one of the few locations where you can still take photographs without any trees blocking the view.

With a wreath of flowers on its front, No. 5029 *Nunney Castle* is seen passing Redhill Curve on 17 February 2015 on its way from Bristol Barton Hill to Crewe HS, sadly to be put into storage.

With a load of eleven coaches, West Coast Railways No. 37706 is seen leaving Hereford on 24 May 2015 with the 5Z67 Bristol Kingsland Road to Steamtown Carnforth ECS.

No. 60085 passes the former St Devereux station on 14 July 2015 with the 6M51 Baglan Bay to Chirk timber working.

After a change of driver, No. 66012 leaves the station on 23 March 2012 with the 6M86 Margam to Dee Marsh steel working. In the summer of 2017, DB closed the driver signing-on point at Hereford station, with around seven drivers losing their jobs and making it rare for a driver change to take place here after many years of drivers and guards being based in Hereford. Freightliner took over the steel workings from Margam to Dee Marsh from DB at the same time but DB still makes an appearance once in a while on the steels. Hereford-based drivers also worked the Hereford to Moreton-on-Lugg stone workings on the last part of their journey. DB still works the trains into and from Moreton and DB are booked to operate some of the night-time freight workings that run through Hereford, but using drivers from other depots.

Just before sunset on a sunny evening, No. 66138 is seen passing Grafton on 12 June 2014 with the 6X52 Portbury to Mossend imported cars working. This working can only be photographed within about six weeks due to the time it arrives in Hereford, which is about 21.00.

Nos 60044 and 60040 are seen passing Grafton on 27 June 2014 with the 6Z60 Arpley Sidings to Margam. Since DB closed the driver signing-on point at Hereford in the summer of 2017, Class 60s are now rare on the Marches Line, with the Class 66s working most of the freight and engineering trains, along with the occasional Colas Class 70s on the Baglan Bay to Chirk timber workings and the odd engineering train.

Going back to a time when BR blue was a common sight, No. 31106 and DRS No. 37682 at the rear are seen passing Haywood on 22 August 2013 with the 1Q13 Newport Alexandra Dock to Hooton test train.

A different view of Hereford station, looking northbound. Due to a new lift being installed, and with the main footbridge closed, a temporary footbridge was put in place by the end of Platform 4. No. 66430 is seen arriving into the station on 29 June 2014 with the diverted 4V38 Daventry to Wentlooge Tesco liner.

Another view taken from the temporary footbridge of a freight train arriving in Hereford in the summer of 2014 is of No. 60001 working the 6V75 Dee Marsh to Margam steel working.

Another view of a train in Hereford features Nos 66040 and 66165 on the 6M60 Newport Alexandra Dock to Bescot clay tanks, passing Lower Bullingham and heading for the station on 21 February 2015. The photograph was taken from Dinedor Hill. I would like to take another photograph from this spot but I fear the area around the track would now be overgrown, and it was a bit of a hike to get to this viewing spot in the first place.

No. 66135 is seen passing Pontrilas on 21 February 2013 with the 6V75 Dee Marsh to Margam train. The photograph was taken from a road bridge and the railway line goes under the road via a small tunnel. I had been informed that the trees had been cut right back and that this view was now back after many years out of service. However, I am sad to report that this view is now covered with trees again, so I am sure this view is now longer available. Pontrilas was the junction for the Golden Valley line to Hay-on-Wye, and in the Second World War Pontrilas had an MOD camp which had a rail link. In the summer of 1997 a siding was used for full timber trains from Arrochar for the local timber company, but this working did not last long and was transferred to Hereford railyard before that closed.

One of the many freight workings using the Marches Line that have lasted is the 6M60 Newport Alexandra Dock to Bescot clay, and No. 66152 is seen passing Redhill on this working on 26 April 2017. There are plans to build housing on this field, so sadly this is another location that I and others have used for many years that may now be lost.

Class 158s have been working the Marches Line for many years, with services from South Wales to North Wales and to Manchester, but I think No. 158763 was the first time a First Great Western Class 158 had travelled on the line. No. 158763 is seen leaving Hereford on 27 September 2013 with the 1Z11 Exeter St Davids to Llandudno.

Class 142s and 143s have been coming to Hereford for many years; most of them have been empty coaching stock, but a few have worked passenger services. Nos 142006 and 143608 are seen leaving Hereford on 10 November 2013 with the 5F40 Craven Arms to Cardiff Canton ECS.

On a sunny morning before most people were up, Nos 37606 and 37611 leave Hereford on their long journey on 30 June 2012 with the 1Z47 Cardiff Central to Scarborough. The buildings and the old railyard are now used by Network Rail and the two sidings are sometimes used by track machines.

No. 70003 is about to enter the tunnel at Haywood, heading for Hereford on 23 April 2013 with the 6M61 Portbury to Rugeley power station train when seen. At one time there used to be three or four coal workings a day from Portbury to Rugeley power station or the power station at Fiddlers Ferry.

No. 67001 is seen leaving Hereford with the 18.21 Cardiff Central to Holyhead train on 2 May 2013. Funded by the Welsh Government, who awarded the contract to Arriva Trains Wales, the working is known as the WAG, with the first service running on 15 December 2008 with a Class 57 and Mark 2 coaches. It now runs with a Class 67 and Mark 3 coaches, Monday to Friday, leaving Holyhead early in the morning and making its return from Cardiff in the late afternoon. It has standard and first-class carriages and has a full dining car. When the Welsh rugby team are playing in Cardiff, the stock is used on a Saturday working from Holyhead to Cardiff to add more seats for passengers travelling from North Wales to Cardiff.

With both engines working, Nos 56078 and 56113 make a fine sound and sight in the spring sunshine as they leave Hereford on 13 May 2013 with the 6M54 Baglan Bay to Chirk Kronospan Colas Rail timber. When this freight runs now, it's with a Class 70.

No. 57305 is looking very smart with its matching coaches when seen passing Grafton in the early morning sunshine on 17 October 2014 with the 1Z60 Swansea to Chester Northern Belle. Class 57s have worked on the Marches Line many times, mainly on railtours and ECS workings with West Coast Railways and with DRS for the Northern Belle. They also worked the Holyhead to Cardiff WAG before Class 67s took over.

GBRf Bardon-liveried No. 66711 passes the college and is about to pass the site of the former Barrs Court Junction signal box on 28 March 2015 with a Pengam Sidings to Croft Quarry working.

GB Railfreight (GBRf) Nos 66743 and 66746 in Royal Scotsman livery wait to leave the station late in the evening of 11 July 2016 with the 1Z78 Bangor to Gloucester leg of the luxury Belmond Royal Scotsman tour of the United Kingdom.

No. 66556, with the last working of the Saturday-only 4V64 Crewe Basford Hall to Wentlooge Freightliner, is seen passing through the station on 31 October 2015.

On a very dull day on 13 December 2015, Nos 56301 and 56098 make a rare sight as they leave Hereford with the 5S56 Plymouth Laira to Kilmarnock HST. The First Great Western stock is going for refurbishment.

DB Schenker No. 66013 is seen passing Grafton on 23 March 2017 with the empty Acton TC to Moreton-on-Lugg tarmac working. The first loaded stone chippings left Moreton-on-Lugg on 16 June 2004. On average, there are ten to fifteen workings a week into and out from Moreton, most of them by EWS, but GBRf have also worked into Moreton, which gave a bit of variety for a period. Sadly, GBRf have now stopped. Empty trains come from Wembley, Acton, Hayles, Southall and Toton, with full ones heading for Hayles and Radlett plus other locations when needed. The empty workings arrive at about 16.15 into Hereford and leave Hereford full around 21.45 to work back. Another empty arrives into Hereford around 21.40 and then works back full around 02.30. All workings travel via Abergavenny and all times are subject to change, and may not work at all on some days.

Just one of the photographs I have taken over the years of a HST around Hereford. No. 43093 arrives in Hereford 3 June 2017 with the 3P31 St Philips Marsh to Hereford empty coaching stock, which will then work the 1P31 Hereford to London Paddington. HSTs took over from Class 47s and 50s and Mark 2 carriages in the late 1980 their days are now numbered with the new Hitachi units coming into service. I will be sorry to see the Class 43 the area as I found that they have given years of good service. Hopefully I will travel to Scotland at some point on them again when they start working services there. Hereford and the Marches Line has another Class 43 w the Network Rail measurement train, which is known as the Flying Banana due to its all-yellow livery and of the Class 43s. One month it works through Hereford with the Crewe CS to Derby RTC via Newport on-Trent and the other month it works the Derby RTC to Swansea Landore via Worcester and Glouceste

A very rare freight working on the Marches Line is seen leaving Hereford with a pair of Direct Rail Services locos, Nos 68033 and 68002, on the 6M63 Bridgewater FD to Crewe coal sidings. DRS diverted via the Marches Line due to engineering work in the Bristol area on 14 September 2017. Hereford has seen Class 68s for a while now on railtours and empty coaching stock, but never on a freight working.

...hi 800 InterCity Express Train (IET) came to Hereford and the Worcester to Hereford line on ...when it worked the 5Z24 Stoke Gifford to Hereford via Worcester. No. 800002 is seen on Platform 2 ...bout to board the train for another platform clearance gauge test around Hereford station. No. 800002 bet... Hereford and Worcester for the day, checking platform clearance gauge and carrying out other tests on 3... ...ck to Stoke Gifford. The first public service of an 800 IET from Paddington to Hereford took place ...017 when a five-car coach unit worked 1W03, the 12.42 Paddington to Hereford.